Finranew

THE BOY WHO SOLD 10 MILLION CRICKETS

AND OTHER CRAZY FACTS ABOUT PEOPLE!

Parachute Press, Inc.
156 Fifth Avenue
New York, NY 10010

Copyright © 1991 Parachute Press, Inc.
ISBN 0-938753-55-X

First printing: October 1991

Printed in the U.S.A.

Illustrations by Steve McInturff
Designed by P. J. Smith

CONTENTS

INTRODUCTION

You might find some of the facts in this book hard to believe—but they're true! That's what's so great about them. All kinds of people do strange and amazing things—from presidents and kings to ordinary kids like you. A genius like Albert Einstein could explain the secrets of the universe, but he couldn't do simple arithmetic! A president of the United States was so afraid of electricity that he refused to touch a light switch! And an ordinary girl in Poland could "see" colors with her fingertips—even when she was blindfolded!

Astound your friends with these fun facts about athletes, outlaws, inventors, superstars, and more. If they don't believe you, you can prove it—just show them this book. We've checked all the facts for you!

LIFE IN THE SPORTS WORLD CAN BE CHANCY. <u>ANYTHING</u> CAN, AND DOES, HAPPEN! THAT'S ONE REASON WHY SO MANY PEOPLE LOVE SPORTS, AND WHY SPORTS ARE FULL OF . . .

ATHLETIC ABSURDITIES

Who was baseball's most unusual pitcher? Fans and sportswriters would have to agree on Hugh Daly. He was in the major leagues for five years in the 1880s. In one no-hitter he struck out 16 men. Back then it took four strikes for a strike-out instead of three. And to think that Daly had only one arm!

No more Mr. Nice Guy! Bailey Howell of the Baltimore Bullets holds the record for personal fouls. During the 1964-65 basketball season he was penalized 345 times!

Talk about a short career! In 1918 Henry Heitman's dream came true when he became the starting pitcher for the Brooklyn Dodgers against the St. Louis Cardinals. It was Heitman's first game in the major leagues and his big chance to make good. The first four Cardinal batters got hits, and Heitman was taken out of the game. The next day he enlisted in the U.S. Navy and never returned to baseball!

What a knockout! In a bout with Eddie Phillips, boxer Jack "The Irish Thrush" Doyle swung so hard he fell out of the ring, bumped his head, and fell unconscious. You could say that Doyle really knocked himself out!

The ice hockey goalie leads a lonely life for about half the game—when the puck is in the opposing team's half of the frozen rink. Armored in heavy protective gear, the goalie stays on his end of the rink, guarding his team's goal. Attacking the other team's goal, far away at the other end of the ice, is his teammates' job—certainly not his! Nevertheless, Ron Hextall, goalie for the Philadelphia Flyers, actually sent the puck into his opponents' goal during the 1986-87 season. He slapped the puck the full length of the rink to score. And when the Flyers were in the post-season play-offs, he did it again!

In the old westerns bad guys wore black. Maybe there's a reason for that! Both the Los Angeles Raiders football team and the Philadelphia Flyers ice hockey team wear black uniforms. They both have the reputation for being the toughest and meanest team in their respective sports! Two psychologists have conducted tests that seem to indicate that teams wearing black are more aggressive and commit more penalties than those wearing other colors!

Pat McGee, a senior at St. Peter's High School in 1937, has gone down in the school's history as a one-man basketball team! In a game between the seniors and sophomores, McGee was the only player on the senior team left in the game when all the rest had fouled out. The score was tied at 32, and there were still over four minutes left to play! Facing the five opposing sophomores all by himself, McGee not only prevented any of them from scoring, but he made three more points—winning the game 35 to 32!

No pitcher could throw a strike to St. Louis Browns' batter Edward Gaedel. Why? Because Gaedel was only 43 inches tall! The St. Louis Browns' owner had brought the midget to the majors to confuse opposing pitchers. Gaedel played only one game on August 15, 1951, and later height requirements prevented any other midgets from playing professional baseball. So Gaedel had a "short" career in more than one way!

Who was the world's most loyal sports fan? It might be the man who attended a football game held in Pullman, Washington, between Washington State and San Jose State back on November 12, 1955. It was a bitter cold 0 degrees, and high winds made it feel even colder. The fan was the only one there! But who was he rooting for? No one stayed around long enough to ask him!

It's well known that famous fighter "Sugar" Ray Leonard borrowed his nickname from fighting great "Sugar" Ray Robinson. But "Sugar" Ray Robinson borrowed his name too! Back during the 1930s young "Sugar" Walker Smith wanted to be a boxer, but he was too young. He borrowed a birth certificate from a friend named Ray Robinson, who was a few years older. In this way, "Sugar" Walker Smith became "Sugar" Ray Robinson!

You're outta here! Bobby Valentine, the manager of the Texas Rangers baseball team, has argued so much that as of July 1, 1991, he has been thrown out of 21 major-league games, by 19 different umpires!

Michael Jordan, basketball superstar for the Chicago Bulls, was <u>cut</u> from his high school basketball team! However, Jordan did make the team the next year, and later played college basketball at the University of North Carolina. He wears his old UNC basketball shorts under his Bulls uniform to remind himself of home.

DEEDS OF DARING ARE PERFORMED BY PEOPLE OF ALL WALKS OF LIFE— NOT ALWAYS ON PURPOSE! THESE ARE SOME OF THE WORLD'S STRANGEST . . .

FANTASTIC FEATS

Long time, no see! Back in 1891, sailor James Bartley fell overboard from his whaling ship, <u>Star of the East</u>. The rest of the crew thought he was lost forever. But later that same day, after capturing a whale and cutting it open, they discovered James Bartley—alive in the whale's stomach!

To tell the tooth . . . The next time you visit the dentist, remember Hans Schaarschmidt. He was in a German jail in 1907 serving time for robbery. The prison was old, and the bars on the window were made of heavy wood. One day, the guards found that Hans had escaped. Investigation showed that he had chewed through the wooden bars!

Fasten your seat belt! That would have been good advice for Captain J.H. Sedley. In 1918 he was a passenger on a Canadian plane that was dodging enemy German gunfire. When the plane flipped over hundreds of feet above the ground, the captain fell out with no parachute. The pilot leveled the plane and flew under the falling man. Sedley landed on the plane's tail, crawled back into his seat, and hung on for dear life until the plane landed safely!

In the 1920s Gertrude Ederle proved that women's physical strength and stamina could no longer be taken lightly. On August 6, 1926, "Trudy" Ederle dived into the English Channel off the coast of France. 14 hours and 31 minutes later, she'd crossed the 35 miles of dangerous water and walked ashore in England. It was the fastest Channel swim ever recorded up to that time—for a man or woman!

Who needs a parachute? In 1944
British Sergeant Nick Alkemade bailed out
of his burning bomber over Germany
without a parachute! He blacked out as
he fell over three miles through the cold
winter night. When he had almost
reached the ground, Alkemade fell
through branches and landed on snow-
covered underbrush. He survived!

In 1942 a United Kingdom Merchant
Navy ship, the S.S. Ben Lomond, was
torpedoed. Second Steward Poon Lim

escaped the sinking ship on a life raft on November 23. He was picked up by a fishing boat on April 5, 1943. He had survived alone on the raft for 133 days—four and a half months—longer than any other person in history!

On October 24, 1901, Annie Taylor became the first person to successfully go over Niagara Falls in a barrel. Who was this female daredevil who conquered the 160-foot waterfall? She was a 43-year-old schoolteacher, and she couldn't swim!

Who is Superman? Maybe it's California Patrolman Clint Collins. In 1965 he heard the cries of 12-year-old Robert Heitsche coming from a West Covina, California, construction site. He found the boy buried beneath a thousand pounds of steel and brick that had collapsed on him. Stooping down, the policeman lifted the half ton of debris off the boy in one quick motion.

People have been able to fly ever since the Wright brothers first took off from Kitty Hawk, North Carolina, in 1903. However, it wasn't until 1986 that anyone flew nonstop around the world. Fliers

Jeana Yeager and Dick Rutan performed that feat aboard their superlight plane the <u>Voyager</u> in nine days, three minutes, and 44 seconds.

Magician Harry Houdini was the greatest escape artist of all time. Once, on a tour of Europe, he was challenged to escape from a safe. He stepped inside, and the door was closed. Houdini was horrified to discover that he was totally unfamiliar with this safe's locking mechanism. He touched the door and it opened! People outside were amazed. Houdini never told them that they'd forgotten to lock the safe!

IN PUBLIC, THEY ARE WORLD LEADERS. IN PRIVATE, THEY MAKE . . .

HYSTERICAL HISTORY

Cleopatra VII, the great Egyptian queen, was not known for her beauty as the movies would have us believe. Actually, it was her intelligence that attracted Julius Caesar and Mark Antony to her. She is believed to have written pamphlets on cosmetics, Egyptian weights and measures, and other scientific subjects.

In 1484 a young explorer came to King John II of Portugal with a theory that the world was round. He wanted the king to sponsor a westward voyage to reach Asia in the east. The king and his royal maritime commission thought the explorer was crazy and rejected his request. The explorer was Christopher Columbus!

Who was the "strongest" king? If you mean strongest smelling, the title might go to Louis XIV, king of France from 1643 to 1715. He hated water and never took a bath. When he did wash, all he cleaned was the tip of his nose!

Catherine the Great was empress of Russia from 1762 to 1796. She was balding and wore a wig. However, she was so afraid that someone would discover this that she imprisoned her hairdresser in an iron cage in her room for three years so he couldn't reveal her secret!

Catherine de Medicis, queen of France in 1547, must have hated fat women. She would not allow any woman in her court to have a waistline of more than 13 inches!

Georges Clemenceau, French prime minister from 1906 to 1909, almost always went to bed with all his clothes on. He'd wear a soft shirt, his coat, his pants—and even his shoes and gloves!

Napoleon Bonaparte, emperor of France from 1804 to 1815, was so upset after losing a battle that he tried to poison himself! But the poison gave him a terrible case of the hiccups, forcing the poison from his stomach and saving his life!

Fidel Castro, the Communist leader of the island nation of Cuba, was an excellent athlete in college. While attending Havana University, he was given a pitching tryout by the U.S. baseball team the Washington Senators (now known as the Minnesota Twins). Think how different history might have been if he had made the team!

One of the most famous sailing ships was the Mayflower, which crossed the Atlantic in 1620, bringing the Pilgrims to the New World. In 1897 the General Society of Mayflower Descendants was formed in memory of their Mayflower ancestors. But they might just as easily have been called the General Society of Speedwell Descendants, since that was the name of the first ship the Pilgrims considered. It proved unseaworthy, however.

The California Gold Rush of 1849 began on John A. Sutter's property when gold was discovered there. However, Sutter was forced into bankruptcy! So many people came and claimed parts of his land that he went broke continually trying to prove in the courts that the land was his!

In hundreds of western movies, American settlers battle Indians as the settlers cross the west in their Conestoga wagons. Ironically, the settlers had named these wagons <u>after</u> an Indian tribe! The wagons were invented in Pennsylvania near an area inhabited by the Conestoga Indians.

IF NECESSITY IS THE MOTHER OF INVENTION, THEN SOME OF THESE SCIENTISTS MUST HAVE BEEN VERY NEEDY! READ ABOUT THE WORLD'S MOST . . .

INVENTIVE INVENTORS

Tricky, tricky! That's what you can call Leonardo Da Vinci, the great sculptor, architect, engineer, and scientist. His secret notebooks were not readable until the early 20th century when someone discovered that his "secret code" was really only backwards writing! The writing could be read only when viewed in a mirror!

Early American writer, patriot, statesman, and inventor Benjamin Franklin is credited with many inventions such as bifocal glasses and central heating. He also invented the very first swimming fins and the rocking chair!

Although he's a famous American hero, few people realize he made the plates to print the first American paper money, he supervised the making of gunpowder for the Continental Army, and he also constructed the boiler for the first ferryboat. Who was he? Paul Revere!

In 1869 William Finley Semple of Mt. Vernon, Ohio, patented a new invention. An article published in a medical journal warned that the invention would "exhaust the salivary glands and cause the intestines to stick together." The invention was chewing gum!

On December 17, 1903, Orville and Wilbur Wright made the first heavier-than-air powered flight—but nobody knew it! The actual date wasn't reported until three years later, after the Wrights had been awarded several patents for their aircraft.

We can all thank Alexander Graham Bell for inventing the telephone. But he should also be remembered as being the man who saved the National Geographic Society from going out of business! When he was 51, Bell became the president of the society. He even paid the magazine's editor out of his own pocket! But his efforts paid off—in 1991 the National Geographic Society celebrated its 103rd anniversary!

Thomas Edison, inventor of the electric light bulb, movies, and the phonograph, was granted more U.S. patents than anyone else. He had 1,093 inventions patented. But some of them were really weird! One was a cigar that stayed lit forever! Another Edison invention was cement furniture! Can you imagine trying to sleep on a concrete bed? At the end of his life, Edison tried to invent a machine that could communicate with the spirits of the dead. Unfortunately, <u>he</u> died before he could finish it.

Albert Einstein was the genius whose theories led to the development of atomic energy. But even though he could explain the secrets of the universe, he couldn't do simple math! He needed his wife's help in filling out his income tax returns since he had trouble adding!

Henry Ford, inventor of the Model T car, was so proud of his invention that he refused to make any improvements on the auto for 18 years. But the car had some obvious problems! To check the gas tank you had to pull out the front seat and stick a ruler down into the tank!

In 1789 George Washington became the first president of the United States. At that time, there was a king of France, an emperor of China, a Russian Czarina, and a Shogun ruler in Japan. Of all those important offices, only the U.S. presidency still exists!

Joseph Merlin, the Belgian inventor who came up with metal-wheeled roller skates, knew how to make an entrance. Merlin decided to unveil his new skates at a big masquerade ball in 1760. He made a dramatic entrance rolling through the door while playing a violin. The only problem was, Merlin didn't know how to stop his skates and crashed right into a huge mirror!

Samuel Langhorne Clemens, who lived from 1835 to 1910, is best known as Mark Twain, author of <u>Tom Sawyer</u>, <u>Huckleberry Finn</u>, and many other famous books. But did you know that in 1871 he also invented suspenders?

CRIMINALS HAVE MADE THEIR MAD
MARKS ON THE PAGES OF HISTORY.
READ ON TO LEARN ABOUT SOME
OF THE STRANGE HABITS AND
UNUSUAL DOINGS OF THESE . . .

LEGENDARY
LAWBREAKERS

Everyone knows that on April 14, 1865, at Ford's Theater in Washington, D.C., actor John Wilkes Booth assassinated President Abraham Lincoln. But did you know that Booth had tried to kidnap President Lincoln three times earlier that same year? He wanted to trade him for the release of Confederate prisoners!

The brothers Frank and Jesse James were the most famous train robbers of the Old West. After one of their robberies they buried more than $1 million worth of gold bars in Oklahoma. After Jesse died, Frank settled down on an Oklahoma farm. He was sure the farm was near the spot where he and his brother had buried the fortune. But, in fact, Frank couldn't remember where they'd buried it. He spent the rest of his life looking for the gold! It's never been found and is probably still there!

Billy the Kid, the young gunfighter of the Arizona Territory of the 1870s, wasn't from the Wild West, and his name wasn't really Billy. It was Henry McCarthy, and he was born on November 23, 1859, in New York City! He died on July 15, 1881, at the age of 21. Although the real number is probably smaller, legend says Billy the Kid killed 21 men, one for each year of his life.

George LeRoy Parker, a native of Beaver, Utah, was taught how to steal horses by a man named Mike Cassidy. George was so grateful to Mike for teaching him this criminal way of life that he began calling himself Butch Cassidy and, with his partner the Sundance Kid, went on to become one of the most famous desperadoes of the Old West.

Chicago's Alphonse "Scarface" Capone was the leading gangster in the United States from 1925 to 1931. His criminal activities included everything from transporting illegal liquor to murder. He was finally convicted and jailed—for not paying any taxes to the government from the money he had earned from his crimes!

George "Machine Gun" Kelly was one of the most famous criminals during the 1930s. Though he committed many crimes, he was convicted of only one, a kidnapping. And he never used a machine gun! Most of his reputation came from his wife, Kathryn, who was fascinated by gangsters. She made up and spread the stories about her husband and made him more famous than his crimes ever did!

Bonnie Parker and Clyde Barrow were two of the most desperate and dangerous bank robbers of the 1930s. The couple would often drive up to a bank in a stolen car, hold up and rob the bank, and then escape by stealing another car. Clyde Barrow preferred Fords to all other cars and actually wrote a fan letter to the Ford Motor Company telling them that he favored their cars because they were fast, had good gas mileage, and were easy to find when he needed to steal one.

Ma, what do we do now? During the gangster days of the 1930s, Clara "Ma" Barker is believed to have led her four sons on a criminal spree that included everything from robbery to kidnapping. Ma Barker was said to have planned the crimes her sons Herman, Lloyd, Arthur, and Freddie carried out. However, after she died, other members of the Barker gang claimed that Ma's criminal activities were just a legend. Instead of planning any crimes, they insisted, Ma was sent off to the movies while her sons robbed banks!

Take from the rich and give to the poor? Charles Arthur "Pretty Boy" Floyd was another famous gangster of the 1930s. Although he killed at least 10 people, he thought of himself as a Robin Hood. He would often sprinkle money out of his getaway car as he and his gang sped away from a bank they had robbed!

WHAT GOES ON BEHIND THOSE WHITE HOUSE DOORS? THE ANSWERS MAY SURPRISE YOU . . .

PRESIDENTIAL PECULIARITIES

Thomas Jefferson, the third president, was so embarrassed that his design for the White House was rejected that he never even told anyone he'd submitted his ideas! He had entered his drawings under a phony name. The secret wasn't discovered until almost a hundred years later when someone found matching drawings in Jefferson's notebooks.

Sarah Polk, wife of 11th president James Polk, believed that dancing was improper. At the Inaugural Ball celebrating her husband's election, all music and dancing stopped when the Polks came in. When they left, two hours later, the dancing and music started up again!

Lyndon Johnson, the 36th president, had a strange way of making sure his friends would remember him—he gave them electric toothbrushes! He said, "Then I know that from now until the end of their days, they'll think of me the first thing in the morning and the last thing at night."

Abraham Lincoln, the 16th president, once had a frightening dream. He reported that in his dream he was walking through the White House and heard people crying. He asked a guard what had happened and was told that the president was dead. A week later, President Lincoln was assassinated!

Grover Cleveland, the 22nd president, had a rubber jaw! In 1893 President Cleveland's jaw was removed because he had

mouth cancer. It was surgically replaced
with one made of vulcanized rubber. This
remained a secret for 24 years!

Electricity was first installed in the
White House in 1891 when Benjamin Harrison, the 23rd president, was in office.
But President Harrison was afraid of electricity! He and his wife would sleep with
the lights on because they were afraid to
touch the light switch!

People liked to refer to Theodore Roosevelt, the 26th president, by the nickname "Teddy." The president was so popular that his nickname was even given to a toy, the teddy bear. But President Roosevelt himself hated the nickname, and nobody close to him would dare call him Teddy!

Does history repeat itself? Consider the assassinations of two of history's most beloved presidents, Abraham Lincoln and John F. Kennedy, which took place 98 years apart. There are some remarkable similarities in the facts surrounding the two men and their assassinations. Lincoln, the 16th president, had a secretary named Kennedy. Kennedy, the 35th president, had a secretary named Lincoln. Both presidents had vice presidents named Johnson. Both men were shot in the back of the head. Both were seated next to their wives when shot. After the shooting, Lincoln's assassin, John Wilkes Booth, ran from a theater and hid in a barn used as a warehouse. Kennedy's assassin, Lee Harvey Oswald, ran from a warehouse and hid in a theater.

You light up my life! Before Richard Nixon became the 37th president, he served two terms as vice-president with President Eisenhower. When Nixon was first elected vice-president, his mother hung a big three-dimensional photo of her son in her stairwell. The photo would light up when she pressed a special button.

As a young man, Ronald Reagan, the 40th president, used to pose for drawing classes at the University of Southern California. The art students voted him "the most nearly perfect male figure!"

President Calvin Coolidge, the 30th president, loved to play practical jokes. One of his favorites was to press all the buttons on his desk and then hide behind his office door. Everyone—secretaries, Secret Service men, White House servants—would race into his office. Then President Coolidge would pop out and say, "I just wanted to see if everyone was working!"

SOMETIMES WEIRDNESS IS A GIFT—A WEIRD GIFT! CHECK OUT THE UNCANNY TALENTS OF . . .

SUPERPOWERED PEOPLE

You've heard of strong man Hercules. You've heard of the powerful Samson. But have you heard of Angus McAskill? This superstrong giant was 7 feet 9 inches tall and weighed 405 pounds—all of it muscle! In 1846, at the age of 21, he traveled with circus great P.T. Barnum and worked with the midget Tom Thumb, who danced on his hand. Angus retired after hurting himself when he was challenged to lift a 2,200-pound anchor! But he didn't get hurt lifting it; it happened when he put it back down again!

Zap! In 1895 it was reported that a girl named Jennie from Sedalia, Missouri, had suddenly become the Electric Girl! Sparks flew from her fingers whenever she reached for metal objects. She also would shock people and animals when she touched them. Just as mysteriously as the power had come, it faded away as the girl got older. Then she was able to lead a normal life.

Back in 1780 Jo Girardelli was known as "The Incombustible Lady" because she was supposedly immune to fire and heat. During her performances she would do such things as swallow acid and hot lead, hold melted sealing wax on her tongue, and touch hot metal to her skin—and she was never hurt. Was it all some kind of trick? Perhaps . . . but no one ever learned how she did her amazing feats.

This guy never needed a light! A.W. Underwood of Paw Paw, Michigan, was a human dragon! It was reported in 1963 that whenever he breathed on a handkerchief, paper, or dry leaves, they burst into flames. Doctors thoroughly examined Underwood and could never find any trickery involved in his amazing fire-breathing power.

It takes long years of study to become a doctor, right? Maybe not. Edgar Cayce completed only the ninth grade, but from 1890, when he was only 13 years old, until his death in 1945, he correctly diagnosed hundreds of diseases and recommended cures while in a trancelike state. Many doctors tried to prove that Cayce, who lived in rural Kentucky, was a fraud, but none succeeded.

In 1973, when she was 10 years old, Bogna Stefanska of Poland could "see" and identify colors with her fingertips. The girl was blindfolded to ensure that she couldn't use her eyes. Scientists call her power "dermo-optical perception," or "skin-sight."

Mathematician Rajan Mahadevan has a fantastic photographic memory. He can remember any number—even 10,672,347,925,772,590,906,000—after seeing it for only a second! However, he sometimes forgets where he put his keys!

Jules Verne, the great French science fiction writer who lived from 1828 to 1905, never claimed to be able to predict the future. His novels <u>Twenty Thousand Leagues Under the Sea</u>, <u>Mysterious Island</u>, and others were just imaginative fiction. However, it turned out that his novel <u>From Earth to the Moon</u> accurately predicted almost every basic detail of the actual first moon landing. Perhaps, without even knowing it, he <u>could</u> see into the future after all!

IT'S NOT EASY BEING FAMOUS—BUT IT SURE CAN BE FUN! THE STARS OF STAGE AND SCREEN ARE CONSTANTLY INVOLVED IN . . .

SUPERSTAR SILLINESS

Don't listen to everything they say! One actor in Hollywood was told by an agent that in order to make it in the movies, he should change his name because his real one was too hard to pronounce. The same agent told the actor that he should take speech lessons to get rid of his Austrian accent. And finally, the agent told the actor that he was just too muscular. The actor ignored the agent's advice. His name? Arnold Schwarzenegger!

There's no denying the fact that movie stars can influence people. Everyone likes to imitate their favorite star. This is just as true today as it was years ago. In 1934 the biggest movie star was Clark Gable. In the Columbia Pictures film <u>It Happened One Night</u>, Gable took off his shirt to reveal he wore no undershirt. Sales of undershirts dropped 40 percent in a few short weeks!

Actor Harrison Ford has starred in some of the highest-grossing films of all time. He played Han Solo in all three <u>Star Wars</u> movies and Indiana Jones in the three films about the heroic archaeologist's adventures. One of his trademarks is a crooked scar below his lower lip. Was it the result of some daring stunt? No! The distinctive scar was due to an auto accident. Ford was trying to put on his seat belt while driving and steered right into a tree!

Johnny Weissmuller was considered the best swimmer in the world after winning a total of five gold medals in the 1924 and 1928 Olympics. But he is better known as Tarzan, King of the Jungle!

Actor Dustin Hoffman really likes to research his roles. In the film <u>Tootsie</u> he played an actor who dresses as a woman so he can get a part in a soap opera. To see if he was convincing, Hoffman put on the disguise and had a long conversation with another actor, Jon Voight. Voight didn't recognize Hoffman at all—even though they knew each other well.

Comedy star Michael J. Fox, star of the Back to the Future films, didn't change his name, but he changed his middle initial. He changed his real middle initial—"A"—to "J" because he didn't want people calling him "Michael, a fox."

Today, writers use computers to keep track of all their work. But back in the 1800s, they had to devise other methods. France's Alexandre Dumas, the author of such classics as The Three Musketeers and The Count of Monte Cristo, used to write all his magazine articles on pink paper, all his poetry on yellow paper, and all his novels on blue paper.

Comedian Jay Leno, the new host of The Tonight Show, was once fired from a job at a Ford dealership after he dropped a stack of hubcaps. When he got home, he wrote a letter to Henry Ford II telling him what had happened. Ford himself called the man who had fired Leno and made him rehire the future comic!

I vant to suck your blood! Movie star Bela Lugosi, the actor most famous for playing the vampire Dracula, loved his role so much that when he died he was buried in his Dracula cape.

Cher, the star singer and Oscar-winning actress, has an easy time remembering her lines for her film performances. Although she was a high school dropout and suffered from dyslexia (a reading problem), she has a photographic memory. She was able to remember all her lines for such films as <u>The Witches of Eastwick</u>, <u>Mask</u>, and <u>Moonstruck</u> after reading each script only once!

In April 1991 rapper M.C. Hammer had an on-the-air argument with comedian Pat Cooper. Cooper didn't like rap music and said M.C. Hammer had no talent. The two argued back and forth until the radio announcer suggested a way for them to settle their differences: a bowling match. A week later Hammer and Cooper met in a New Jersey bowling alley. Cooper won the match, and the two left as friends.

Have you ever heard of the rock group Vengeance K.S.A.? They might not have had a hit record, but they hold the record for marathon playing. From September 7 to September 11, 1987, this four-piece heavy-metal English rock band played for 107 hours nonstop!

Paul Simon is one songwriter who gets his inspiration in unusual places. He was in an all-night diner when the name of a dish on the menu inspired one of his best-known songs. The dish was made of chicken and eggs. The dish—and Simon's song—was called "Mother and Child Reunion."

M.C. Hammer, whose real name is Stanley Kirk Burrell, was once a batboy for the Oakland A's! Charles Finley, the owner of the team, hired Hammer when he saw him dancing in the parking lot of the Oakland Coliseum. The players called him "Hammer" because he looked like "Hammerin' Hank"—Hank Aaron, one of baseball's all-time great hitters.

YOU DON'T HAVE TO BE AN ADULT TO DO ZANY THINGS. SOMETIMES THE WACKIEST PEOPLE ARE . . .

THOSE CRAZY KIDS

The famous tune to "Twinkle, Twinkle, Little Star" was written by a six-year-old! Wolfgang Amadeus Mozart, one of the world's greatest composers, wrote the music in 1762.

Can you imagine a teenage girl terrifying the entire world! It's true! A seventeen-year-old girl wrote a book in 1818 that is still scaring people today! The girl was Mary Shelley, and the book was <u>Frankenstein</u>!

Back in 1904, teenager Mildren Wallace baffled her parents and doctors with her amazing journeys. She claimed that she could send her mind out of her body while in a trance and travel anywhere in the world. Her doctor tested her. Before he left his office for her home many miles away, he left a medical textbook opened to a specific page on his desk. At Mildren's home, he asked her to mentally "travel" to his office and read the page number of the open book. When Mildren woke up, she told the startled doctor the exact page!

Edwin Booth was a kid who had a lot to live down. His father, John Wilkes Booth, assassinated President Abraham Lincoln. Perhaps he felt better when he remembered a heroic feat he performed two years before his father's notorious act. Standing on a train platform, Edwin had saved the life of another boy who almost fell in front of an oncoming train. The boy he saved was Robert Lincoln—President Lincoln's son!

Sweet dreams! An 11-year-old boy from Danville, Illinois, had a long sweet one in 1988. When his mother discovered him missing one morning, she told police that the boy walked in his sleep. The police found the boy sleepwalking along railroad tracks in Peru, Indiana, a hundred miles from Danville. He had climbed on board a freight train and traveled in his sleep!

Back in 1933 two teenage boys living in Cleveland, Ohio, thought up what they believed to be a terrific comic strip. Jerry Siegel wrote it, and his friend Joe Shuster drew it. For five years the strip was rejected by every editor in the business. They told the boys that their character was "too fantastic" and that nobody would believe in him. Finally, in 1938, the strip was published in a new format called a "comic book." The character was Superman!

It was reported in 1980 that Kipp Hockin of Farwell, Michigan, learned single-handedly how to harvest crickets! He'd shake the crickets out from where they roosted and put them in boxes to be mailed to bait shops. Kipp and his family sold about 10 million crickets a year!

Jason Bright of Hope, Arkansas, must have the greenest thumb in the state—and maybe in the world. In 1989 he grew the world's largest watermelon! It weighed 260 pounds—more than Jason's father!

No kidding, what a kid! In 1962 Dorothy Straight became an author when Pantheon Books bought and published her picture book, <u>How the World Began</u>. So what? Well, Dorothy was only four years old! She thus became the youngest recorded commercially published author of all time!

Bubble gum is a favorite treat of Susan Montgomery Williams of Fresno, California. In 1989 she achieved the world's record for blowing the largest bubble gum bubble. It measured 22 inches in diameter.

It was certainly "in the cards" for John Sain back on August 3, 1983, when he was 15 years old. He built the tallest playing-card tower on record. It stood 12 feet 10 inches high. None of the 15,714 cards were creased or folded, and no glue of any kind was used.

READ ALL ABOUT IT! HERE ARE BIZARRE, UNUSUAL, AND AMAZING FACTS ABOUT SOME . . .

WONDROUS WOMEN

101, 102, 103, 104. . . counting sheep never helped Ines Fernandez. In 1973 it was reported that Señora Ines Fernandez had not slept for 30 years! She told doctors that one day in 1943, she yawned and felt a sharp pain in her head. Since that day, she has not slept at all!

Legend has it that in the year 1040 Lady Godiva rode naked through the Coventry marketplace in England on a white horse. She was supposedly protesting her husband's overtaxing of his people. There really was a Lady Godiva, she really did object to her husband's taxing of the people, and people still celebrate her famous ride. Only one problem: It never happened!

The Flying Nun! When Mary Hargrafen became a nun as a member of the Sisters of St. Francis, she was known as Sister Mary Carl. However, in 1978 she was also known as Captain Mary Hargrafen. As a member of the U.S. Air Force, she was the first nun to become a U.S. Air Force captain!

Florence Nightingale, the founder of modern nursing, was so dedicated to her profession that she willed her body to medical science. However, when she died in 1910, her friends couldn't bring themselves to let her body be dissected, even for noble purposes. She was buried, intact.

Aviator Amelia Earhart was the world's greatest female flier in the early days of aviation. She was the first woman to duplicate Charles Lindbergh's feat of flying solo across the Atlantic. But she also attained firsts of her own. In January

1935 she became the first person ever to fly from Hawaii to North America (she landed in Oakland, California). In April of the same year she became the first to fly from Los Angeles to Mexico City. Three weeks later she flew from Mexico City to Newark—another first!

Susan B. Anthony was an American reformer and leader of the women's suffrage movement. In 1872 she was arrested and fined. Her crime? She'd <u>voted</u> in the 1872 presidential election—women were not allowed to vote in federal elections until 1920.

In 1989 Kristin M. Baker, a female student at the U.S. Military Academy at West Point, became First Captain of the Corps of Cadets, the highest honor the Academy can bestow. But the real reason Kristin Baker is important is because it wasn't until 1976 that West Point allowed women to attend. Ms. Baker was the first female cadet captain in the Academy's 187-year history!

Anna Mary Robertson Moses was born in 1860. Around 1937, in her late 70s, she began painting rural scenes. The primitive paintings caught the attention of members of the Museum of Modern Art in New York. "Grandma" Moses went on to gain worldwide fame and continued painting until she was over 100 years old!

Give her a hand! At 4 feet 9 inches tall and 95 pounds, Lillian Leitzel was an acrobat for the Ringling Brothers Barnum & Bailey Circus. In 1918 she had a bet that she could break the one-handed chin-up record of 12 chin-ups in a row, which had been set by a man. She astounded everyone by doing 27 chin-ups with her right hand. Then, to everyone's amazement, she did 19 chin-ups with her left!

The most successful recording artist of all time is a woman—and no, it's not Madonna. It's Jane Barbe. Never heard of her? Here's one of her hits: "At the tone, the time will be. . . ." She's the voice that tells you the correct time over the telephone. AT&T estimates that Jane Barbe's recordings are played over 25 trillion times a year!

Phone home! In 1944 Aimee Semple McPherson, an evangelist and faith healer, was buried with a live, working phone in her coffin! Maybe her friends wanted a call from the afterlife!